Cannabis Cookbook

The Essential Guide to Edibles and Cooking with Marijuana

Eva Hammond

and

Aaron Hammond

By Eva Hammond and Aaron Hammond

Version 1.1

Published by HMPL Publishing at KDP

Get to know your publisher and his work

www.facebook.com/HMPL-publishing

A Note from the authors

It has been a pleasure to write this book. This book is a project of me and my wife, where she collected the recipes and shared some of her kitchen secrets. With my knowledge and experience with cannabis edibles, and both our passion for cannabis combined, we created this essential guide for edibles and marijuana infused cooking. We bring you some of the classics from the American cuisine. well mostly snacks and comfort foods to make them yourself. We try to provide you with the essential knowledge to make edibles and cannabis infused cooking as this comes down to responsible use and education.

We hope that you will enjoy this book and make use of the provided 40 plus recipes that we have presented you! Stay tuned as Eva will work on more books regarding recipes and cannabis cuisine.

Much Love and kind regards,

Eva & Aaron Hammond

damage, or monetary loss due to the information herein, either directly or indirectly.

Table of Contents

Bonus

Welcome to HMPL Publishing! Let's start right away with an exclusive bonus made available only for our inner circle. Get your free copy of 'The best DIY THC & CBD recipes to prepare at home' **http://eepurl.com/cxpVZf**

Subscribing to our newsletter will guarantee you with the latest THC and CBD recipes, articles and some of our upcoming books for absolutely free. To make that even better we'll update you with the most recent information about Marijuana, medical breakthroughs and the various applications of cannabis.

Subscribe to the HMPL Publishing newsletter, and we'll give you our free THC & CBD recipes to prepare at home book for free.

All you have to do is enter your email address to get instant access.

We don't like spam and understand you don't like spam either. We'll email you no more than 2 times per week. Here are some of the things you can expect as a subscriber to HMPL Publishing's newsletter:

- The latest books by HMPL Publishing, exclusive and free for subscribers

- Delicious recipes to prepare in the comfort of you own kitchen

- Exclusive marijuana-related lectures, articles and information

- Special discounts for detailed eBooks about marijuana

- And much, much more...

To subscribe, go to **http://oopurl.com/cxpV7f**

Delicious world of edibles

The cannabis industry is rising and I am very lucky to contribute my part of sharing knowledge about this amazing herb. My field of expertise lies within the world of health and nutrition as I passed for my bachelor's degree at the University of Wageningen. Food and health always sparked my interest and I am a big supporter of everything in moderation. I don't want to make this book about which diet or choice of food is the best for your health. This is but a sheer essential guide to the world of edibles and cooking with marijuana. The basics of properly decarbing your product and infused it with oil or butter is fundamental to potent edibles. But we are not there yet; I would say that proper information about the starting product cannabis is the key to making the most out of your infused cooking endeavours.

Topics regarding the basics about marijuana are just as important as the recipes as you're dealing with a potent medicine which could offers you great potential but also kick you in the face if you're not being careful. By this I mainly point at dosing your cannabis for ingestion because it is a whole different world compared to smoking or vaporizing your bud. Simply put, the active compounds in cannabis have a stronger effect if they enter your body through your digestive system. This offers great medical potential but what would normally be a pleasant amount for smoking can turn your world upside down if you're inexperienced when it comes to edibles. I cannot stress this enough and you'll read it many times throughout this book. Basic principle; smoking tolerance is definitely not the same as edible tolerance, Smoking about 200 mg of THC might be a walk in the park as a figure of speech for an experienced smoker but if you never had a strong edible, 200mg of THC will blast you off into outer space. This could potentially be a very uncomfortable situation and it wouldn't be the first time someone ending up on IC thinking they'd overdosed on pot brownies. I am no stranger to such effects; edibles are my choice to go right now but I miscalculated it sometimes in the past and got some unpleasant experiences under my belt. But we'll talk later about these topics when it comes to dosing, potency and harm reduction for potential bad experiences.

An introduction to cannabis and edibles

Cannabis has been known in humanity for a long now with the earliest recorded use of cannabis around 3000 BC in north-eastern parts of china and region north eastern of what is now known as Russia and Siberia, The earliest use for cannabis has been found within ancient Chinese civilization, where stories explain the medical position of cannabis as an anaesthetic for surgery in their society and some even tell us that one of the first Chinese emperors called Shen Nung already used cannabis for his own pleasure.

Hemp known as Cannabis Ruderalis and varieties of cannabis sativa and indica crossed the planet over the next centuries, travelling the globe from China through India and arriving in Europe around the 5th century. People discovered hemp seeds on Viking ships for officially cannabis took over the American continent by the 19th century.

We won't go much into detail as I elaborated more on the specifics of cannabis use throughout time in one of my earlier books on Cannabis extracts, but I do want note that the earliest use of cannabis by oral ingestion started within those Asian societies and had a major impact in India. Most of the earliest documented recipes come from India as Bhang dates back to 2000BC and still has a place in Indian festivals such as Holi, Janmashtami and Shivrati and consuming bhang at such occasions is common. This is also legal in India as it serves an important role in India's culture and spiritual practices and it would be impossible to criminalize cannabis completely in the country.

With legalization for cannabis and 29 states in the US that gave green light for at least medical use, the western world with an illicit stigma around cannabis propagated by the media is changing fast. I consider myself an activist for legalization and I think information and education is the key to achieve that. But enough about that, you're reading this because you want to cook and although a bit of personal information is always appreciated we should get to the point of this book.

Cannabis is mainly known for its two major compounds known as THC and CBD and with about 113 other active compounds. I won't into any of the plants biology stuff as I've written other books about it and if you want to learn in a formal, objective but easy to understand way about cannabis and how it works I recommend you to check out my other books.

THC, CBD and other Cannabinoids

phytocannabinoids such as CBD or THC is a one of a class of diverse chemical compounds that are found within cannabis and hemp plants, to be exact; this is only found in the resin that the buds or the flowers of the cannabis plants produces, and can be found within the glistering resin on buds, spreading out on the surrounding leaves and stalks. This resin contains all of the magic; such as the cannabinoids known for their effects on our body and a vast array of terpenes that make up for the taste. Terpene pairing with food is considered to be the high cuisine of cannabis and in due time I would love to research that. But focusing on the plant material for edibles; you can use resinous leaves and stalks and leftover bud material such as trimmings for edibles, I am secretly a big fan of using flower as this will make your product kick ass.

We'll discuss dosing and measurements later but let's say you buy a gram of top shelf tested at 23% THC; you're looking at 230 mg of THC and with a conversion rate of an estimated 0.88 by infusion, if you do it properly you should be able to extract about 202 mg of THC from that gram, which would potentially be about 8 doses of 25 mg THC which is a definitely something that will get you higher than smoking 1/8 of gram, But we're bound to an efficiency rate for infusion that is about 60% so more about that in the actual chapter regarding this subject.

So enough about that but I just wanted to mention the fact that edibles are actually worth it, considering that smoking the same amount of bud wouldn't last me a day.

Back to cannabinoids, these compounds act on cannabinoid receptors in cells that alter your neurotransmitter release in the brain such as THC alters the release of the neurotransmitter called dopamine also known as the 'feel good' chemical.

The endocannabinoid system

The human brain has multiple cannabinoid receptors known as the endocannabinoid system whereas two receptors found within the endocannabinoid system are currently identified as CB1 and CB2; these two cannabinoid receptors are also common in animals; you can find them in mammals, birds, fish, and reptiles.

Cannabinoid receptors type 1

As a part of the endocannabinoid system, Cannabinoid receptors type 1 are primarily found in the brain, more specifically found in the basal nuclei part of the brain and in your limbic system, including the hippocampus. They are also found in the cerebellum and in both male and female reproductive systems which accounts for a variety of effects once THC for example by affecting these receptors, using a high THC product can give a relatively potent effect, giving patients significant relief from pain, nausea, or depression while delivering a strong euphoria to lifestyle users.

Cannabinoid receptors type 2

Cannabinoid receptors type 2 are predominantly found in our immune system or immune derived cells with the greatest density in the spleen. While only found in the peripheral nervous system; the peripheral nervous system runs throughout our body to connect our limbs and organs to the central nervous system which is found in the brain and spinal cord. So it acts as a line of communication between the brain and spinal cord with the rest of the body. CB2 receptors seem to be responsible for the anti-inflammatory effects and possible other therapeutic effects of cannabis.

Cannabis as a medicine

Researchers continue to study the medical benefits of cannabis. Over time there have numerous researches that showed how cannabis is effective at treating cancer and many other diseases and conditions, I will have to include a list with publications of diverse researches and clinical trials about the effects of cannabis on cancer that have been published on the US government website for US National Library of Medicine National Institutes of Health and Bio technology so you can see for yourself what the facts are.

Here is a list of what cannabis is known to be able to treat:

- **Chronic pain**, *due of its effect on the central nervous system*

- **Nausea**

- **Muscle spasms**, *especially those associated with certain conditions, such as multiple sclerosis*

- **AIDS**, *It is not a cure for aids as far as we know right now but it offers great relief for patients suffering from AIDS or HIV*

- **Anorexia**

- **Arthritis**

- **Cachexia**

- **Cancer**, *the PubMed list will actually prove that there are substantial results for cannabis as a cure for cancer.*

- **Depression**

- **Anxiety**

- **Fibromyalgia**

- **Parkinson's Disease**

- **Alzheimer**, Cannabis has been proven to slow the aging process of the brain

- **COPD**

- **Glaucoma**

- **Migraine**, *I experienced this first hand, it doesn't take away all the pain but it helps you sleep through it and makes it quite bearable.*
- **Seizures**, *including those related to epilepsy*
- **Severe nausea**

Medical marijuana is commonly used to treat certain symptoms with great results, especially in people suffering from listed conditions and diseases.

Edibles are a great way to medicate with cannabis, and definitely my go to for day to day medication and we'll start off with dosing and measuring your edibles.

Dosing and measuring your edibles.

Dosing your edibles can be super tricky but if you gain some experience over time as I cooked many batches of edibles and sometimes had to learn through shameful and uncomfortable experiences where I took too much and it kicked me in the head. Getting it exactly right is nearly impossible, as I tried edibles from several dispensaries and even there if I bought a bad of THC infused salted popcorn, the potency can vary a lot, it might say a 1000 mg on the bag and the bag contains a 1000 mg of THC that doesn't mean that if you eat a piece it is always going to be the same strength and exactly the same measurements. You will notice this especially if you have a low tolerance for edibles and we will get into that with the chapter; the right way to edibles. So here we have the key points to dosing your edibles;

- Check the label before you extract if you buy it from a dispensary. Measuring without knowing your bud is a lost cause. Some producers note THC percentage on flower packaging, while others note THCA. If you see a THCA percentage, use the 0.88 conversion rate to determine potential THC.

- Portion your cannabutter vertically. "Gravity impacts everything," says Davidson, "and each cannabinoid has a different molecular weight, so they will settle in different places." Butter from the bottom of the batch will be different than butter from the top, so don't scoop straight off the top.

- Measure carefully if you have to make single batch doses. Don't plop a big spoonful of cannabutter into the batter, get yourself some measuring cups, and fill and level them precisely.

- Stir well. The next best thing is to stir until you're positive the batter is perfectly homogenous and then stir some more

- Portion your dough batter or other product evenly, if you did the last step you get a more precise dosing if you measure your portion evenly.

- Plan on variation of potency but be careful. If you find out that your edibles are not even close in potency I urge you to be very careful with eating more then you initially should as you could end up having an uncomfortable experience.

Calculating edible potency

If I have 100g of top-shelf Casey Jones. I would estimate the potency around approximately 20%, or about 200mg THCA per 1g of bud. So this means that 200mg of THCA x 100 is 20,000mg THCA.

The conversation from THCA to THC is 0.88 as I mentioned earlier. So this would mean that 20,000mg x 0.88 = 17,600mg maximum THC available to be extracted.

Under the ideal conditions, you would get a 60% efficiency of extraction in butter, so that means 17,600mg x 0.6 = and you're looking at 10,560mg maximum THC likely to be extracted.

So with this knowledge if your targeted dosage is 200mg per brownie, then 10,560mg / 200 = 53 brownies that contains around 200mg each. This is the maximum those brownies will have; they could potentially have a lot less depending on the infusion process and if that is done properly.

The right way to edibles

The right way to edibles is in the dosing, no matter how much you hear it, no matter how much you're going to read it in this book, I can't stress this enough. It all starts out with picking the right strain for your edible, when it comes to cannabis and effect we have to start at the basics for strains, we got three types of strains; sativa, indica and hybrids. Hybrids are crosses between sativa and indica strains and are indicated by percentage, ranging from 50/50 to 70/30 and are either sativa or indica dominant, even with a 50/50 cross you can still feel the difference; for example S5 haze is a 50/50 hybrid but has a strong and dominant uplifting sativa effect to it which fades away over time into a more relaxing indica state of mind. Even though it is classed as a 50/50 I would say that it feels sativa dominant. That's also where we get into effects the effects of sativa and indica strains.

Indica strains are known to have great medical potential and they are very effective for overall pain relief and stress relief. You can benefit from indica strains to treat insomnia and increase their appetites. Indica buds are most commonly smoked by medical marijuana patients in the late evening or even right before bed due to how sleepy and tired you become when high from an indica strain of marijuana. The most popular Indica strains currently include several strains like Bubba Kush, Blueberry and Northern Lights.

Sativa-dominant provides an uplifting, energetic and more cerebral high that is best suited for daytime use. A sativa high is filled with creativity and energy as being high on sativa can spark new ideas and creations. It offers great medical potential to patients that suffer from ADHD and COPD as well as people that benefit from cannabis in general because sativa strains can help you get through the without the couch-lock from indica strains.

So when it comes to edibles the effects depend on the strain but here are 5 tips that are the key to comfortable and fun edible experience.

1. Read the label or know your estimated dose

Whether you bought them at your local dispensary or you're about to eat some homemade cookies, you have to make sure that you know what you're getting yourself into, A good dose to start with when you're completely new to cannabis would 5mg of THC, for someone who has never done edibles but has some experience with cannabis this would be10 mg of THC, for medical use you can start out a little higher depending on your condition but the absolute maximum would 25 mg for a first time experience.

2. Start off slow

Edibles react with your system in a different way than some good old fashioned smoking. This comes from the fact that the THC absorbs through your stomach lining, before entering your bloodstream to travel to the brain. This means that it takes time before you feel the effects of cannabis and it can take up to 90 minutes or more in some cases, usually effects are felt within an hour but don't just eat more if you don't feel anything. If it is your first time, start out with a very small dose and two hours later you can decide whether to take more or not.

3. Keep it separate from the snacks

This one is very important as you wouldn't be the first that cooks up some very tasty edibles and when the munchies kick in, you suddenly realize everything is gone and in the best case scenario you wake up about 20 hours later when they kick in, depending on how much you made of course. So keep them away and buy some regular snacks.

Keeping it put away will also prevent anyone else from accidentally eating your edibles and having an unexpected trip of their own.

4. Don't mix and match

The safest bet when trying edibles is to stick with one thing at a time. You might feel the urge to smoke a few bowls waiting for the edible to start working, but when it hits, you might have too much THC in your system at once. This goes double for using more than one edible at a time. Double dosing is for seasoned edible users only.

5. Take care of yourself

Edibles, since they go through the stomach, can affect each person differently.

And on an empty stomach you're wasting your edibles as your liver will breakdown most of the THC before it reaches your intestines meaning your edible will lose most of its effect on an empty stomach. So the best thing to do is to get a good meal down at least an hour before you start on your edible.

7 tips if you had too much

The moment where your cannabis edible finally kicks in... It can sometimes be a scary moment if you're not prepared or if it turns out to be stronger than you had anticipated. Not to worry, thankfully Mother Nature offers us a few reset buttons if you over medicate.

1. Calm Down and Relax: I know you just ate your whole batch of No Bake fudge, but rest assured freaking out and panicking is only going to make it worse. Try meditation techniques paired with deep breathing exercises to replace the panic thoughts, which will allow you to calm yourself.

2. Find a quiet setting: Bright visual stimuli, loud noises, crowds of people can all add to the disorientation you experience during a THC high. Coupled with the first item on this list, finding a quiet place to "cool out" is one of the better ways to collect yourself when you're out in public or away from home.

3. Hydrate while you medicate: Cottonmouth isn't a joke and while you're medicating, the body's need for water intake increases. A nice cold glass of water will help refresh and rejuvenate, while also helping prevent severe headaches.

4. Increase your Blood Sugar Levels: Cannabis has been associated with lowering or regulated blood sugar levels in the body. Eating fruits or anything with a natural sugar content will help to reduce the effects of your THC high.

5. Take CBD: Ingesting CBD counteracts the psychoactive effects of THC by way of a sedative effect. A higher level of CBD will work to balance out your feelings associated with the THC high.

6. The Black Pepper Trick: Terpenes are the wonderfully aromatic oils that plants/fruits produce naturally. These oils have natural medicinal properties that when paired with cannabis, work together to provide a number of different affects for users. Black Pepper contains a terpene named Beta-Caryophyllene which can be used to treat anxiety or depression and also induce drowsiness. Just chewing 2-3 black peppercorns can help to reduce the effects from overmedicating.

7. Try to sleep: Sleeping is the most effective way to remedy smoking or ingesting too much cannabis. Even though edibles take longer to digest and be processed, the grogginess you'll feel upon awakening will subside with time as you go through your day.

Decarboxylation and why is this absolutely necessary?

Decarboxylation is turning your non-psychoactive THCA into THC for short. But if we go into explanation of this process you have to start the fact that all cannabinoids contained within the trichomes and resin of raw cannabis flowers have an extra carboxyl ring or group known as COOH attached to their chain. For example, THCA or tetrahydrocannabinolic acid is synthesized within the trichome heads of freshly harvested cannabis flowers. In most regulated markets right now; cannabis distributed in dispensaries contains labels detailing the product's cannabinoid contents. THCA, in many cases, prevails as the highest cannabinoid present in items that have not been decarboxylated such as buds or hash and certain extractions.

THCA has a number of known health and medicinal benefits when consumed, including anti-inflammatory and neuro-protective qualities. But THCA is not psychoactive, and must be converted into THC through decarboxylation before any effects can be felt.

The two main reasons for decarboxylation to occur are heat and time. Drying and curing cannabis over time will cause a partial decarboxylation to occur. This is why some cannabis flowers also test for a presence of small amounts of THC along with THCA. Smoking and vaporizing will instantaneously decarboxylate cannabinoids due to the extremely high temperatures present, making them instantly available for absorption through inhalation.

While decarboxylated cannabinoids in vapor form can be easily absorbed in our lungs, edibles require these cannabinoids present in what we consume in order for our bodies to absorb them throughout digestion. Heating cannabinoids at a lower temperature over time allows us to decarboxylate the cannabinoids while preserving the material so you can infuse into your oil or butter to make edibles.

The THCA in cannabis begins to decarboxylate at approximately 220F after around 30-45 minutes of exposure. Full decarboxylation may require some more time to occur. I would choose to decarboxylate their cannabis at slightly lower temperatures for a much longer period of time in attempts to preserve terpenes. Making up for some of the characteristics in taste of your flower, and also gives the indication of what you're eating actually tastes a bit green.

Heat and time can also cause other forms of cannabinoid degradation to occur. For example, CBN (cannabinol) is formed through the degradation and oxidization of THC, a process that can occur alongside decarboxylation. CBN accounts for a much more sedative and less directly psychoactive experience.

In order to decarboxylate cannabis at home, all you need is some starting material, an oven set to 220-23 F (depending on your location and oven model), some parchment paper, and a baking tray. Finely grind your cannabis until the material can be spread thin over parchment and placed on your baking sheet. Allow the cannabis to bake for 45-60 minutes, or longer if would want that

Always decarb your bud before you go for infusion in oil butter or another solvent, because even though part of that process happens though simmering your product, it has been tested that this comes nowhere close to the full potential of your material.

Clarified Butter (Ghee)

Clarified butter is used when you'll be frying or cooking something either for an extended period or over high heat. For those times when you want the flavor of butter, rather than oil, you'll want to use clarified butter can stand being cooked longer, and to a higher temperature, than regular butter. Clarifying butter removes the milk proteins and water, which are what causes butter to burn if cooked for a long time. This ideal for infusing your cannabutter as you will need to simmer this for over an hour usually and regular butter easily burns over extended periods of simmering especially with flower in it.

Ingredients:

- Unsalted butter, cut into cubes

Tools:

- Heavy Sauce pan

- Spatula

- Fine steel strainer

- Cheese cloth

- Heat Proof container

Procedure:

1. Heat the unsalted butter in a heavy-duty saucepan over very low heat, until it's melted. Let simmer gently until the foam rises to the top of the melted butter. The butter may splatter a bit, so be careful.

2. Once the butter stops spluttering, and no more foam seems to be rising to the surface, remove from heat and skim off the foam with a spoon.

3. Line a fine steel strainer with a few layers of cheesecloth or gauze, and set the strainer over a heatproof container.

4. Carefully pour the warm butter through the cheesecloth-lined strainer into the container, leaving behind any solids from the bottom of the pan.

Note: Clarified butter will keep for 3 to 6 months in the refrigerator. Some say you can leave it at room temperature if the conditions are optimal, but I keep mine under refrigeration. It can also be frozen for a longer length of time.

Double boiler method

When you put a pot on the stovetop, it gets hot especially the parts of the pot that make physical contact with the heating element, but for cannabis infusion this is not always the best way to go as depending on your stove, thing might get too hot to quickly, if your using normal dairy butter instead of clarified butter this can result in burning your butter in mere seconds, and for clarified butter the burning point in much higher but you might get your oil too hot and lose THC in the process as this will vaporize. So the double boiler method gives the perfect opportunity to let your infusion simmer for hours around boiling point without getting to hot too fast and is easier to regulate just by adding cold water in the bottom pot.

A double boiler consists of a bowl or a smaller pot placed on top of a pan of simmering water. The bowl doesn't have to touch the water, but creates a seal with the bottom pan to trap the steam produced by the simmering water. The trapped steam keeps the top bowl going at just about 212F (100C), the temperature at which water turns to steam and a far lower temperature than could be achieved by putting the bowl directly on that burner. Inside the top bowl, you can melt chocolate without worrying that it will stick and burn.

You can buy a double boiler, but it's easy to make one at home. All you need to make a double boiler is a mixing bowl (glass/Pyrex or metal) and a saucepan that the bowl will fit on top of. The two should fit tightly together; you don't want a gap between the bowl and the saucepan, nor do you want a bowl that sits precariously on a tiny saucepan. To use the double boiler, add water to the pan and bring it to a simmer, then place the bowl on top and fill it with whatever you intend to cook or melt.

Cannabutter

Ingredients:

1/2 oz. flowers

8 oz. clarified butter

Tools:

- Sheet pan

- Crock pot or double boiler method

- Fine Steel Strainer

- Cheese Cloth

Procedure:

1. Preheat oven to 220°F.

2. Grind your flowers down in a blender or food processor. Spread ground flower evenly on bottom of a sheet pan and place in middle of oven.

3. Bake for an hour, stirring once halfway through. Make sure the flower stays evenly spread out.

4. Take pan out of oven and allow it to cool down for 10 minutes.

5. Let flowers sit for 10 to 15 minutes. Meanwhile, begin melting your butter over low heat.

Since you have already decarboxylated, the butter only needs to be hot enough to extract cannabinoids. A slow simmer is good. Spoon the flower into the butter and stir. Extract using a Crock Pot or the double boiler method set on low for 6 hours and stir every hour or so to prevent burning.

6. Once your infusion is done, turn off heat and let the cannabutter cool down for at least 20 minutes.

7. Line a metal strainer with cheesecloth. Pour your butter through the cheesecloth and use a spoon to squeeze all the infused cannabutter out.

8. Now your cannabutter is ready to use in our recipes! Keep it in the fridge and use within two weeks or put it in the freezer and it will last you for about 4-6 months

Canna-Oil

Ingredients:

- 6 cups olive oil

- 1 ounce cannabis buds, finely ground, or 2 ounces of trimmed leaf, dried and ground, Decarbed.

Tools:

- Heavy Sauce Pan or double boiler method

- Spatula

Procedure:

1. In a heavy saucepan or a double boiler, slowly heat oil on low heat for a few minutes.

2. You should begin to smell the oil's aroma. Add a little bit of cannabis to the oil and then stir until it is fully coated with oil.

3. Keep adding more cannabis until the entire amount of cannabis is mixed into the oil. Simmer on low heat for 45 minutes, stirring occasionally.

4. Remove the mixture from the heat and allow it to cool before straining. Press the cannabis against a metal strainer with the back of a spoon to wring all the oil out of it.

5. The oil is best stored in an airtight container in the refrigerator for up to 2 months.

Cannabis infused coconut oil: The long method

Ingredients:

Note: Make sure you got time for this as the process can take up 16-20 hours!

- Organic unrefined Coconut Oil

- 1-3 Ounces of dried and decarbed cannabis

  Water

Tools:

- Crockpot

- Fine Metal Strainer

- Coffee grinder

- Cheese Cloth

- Large container

- Thermometer

Pro tip: if you want to have less of a weed scent and taste to your final product leave your buds soaked in water overnight

Procedure:

1. Grind the cannabis extremely fine. A coffee grinder works great, but make sure not to get it too powdery. This will make it harder to strain out in the final process.

2. In the crockpot, add the coconut oil and enough water to float the oil in the pot.

3. Set the heat on high and allow the oil to liquefy.

4. Slowly start stirring in the bud until the mixture is completely saturated. If needed, add more water.

5. Stick a thermometer in the pot with the lid closed on top, and monitor this closely it until it reaches close to 250F. Turn the crockpot heat setting to low and stir.

NOTE: Oil continues to rise in temperature after removed from heat, and takes longer to start cooling. So try to pre-emptive heat switch because this will help you keep a more accurate temperature.

7. Periodically stir the mixture and check that the temperature stays around 250 - 270 degrees.

Note: An occasional flip from low heat to hot may be needed to regulate the temp.

9. The mixture needs to stay below 320 degrees to avoid burning off the active ingredient. The water in the pot stops this from happening because it will evaporate first.

10. Periodically add water throughout the process to keep the cannabis submerged.

11. After 12 - 18 hours, turn off the crockpot and allow it to cool for a while.

12. Get the cheesecloth and double wrap it over your strainer. Place over a large container to catch the warm liquid.

13. Slowly pour the mixture into the cheesecloth and allow dripping. If it's not too hot, wrap the plant material and squeeze out the hot oil

14. Continue until all the mixture has been squeezed out of the cheese cloth.

15. The remaining plant material can be saved to use for a topical compress. Although most of the medicinal properties lie within the oil still trapped in the spent bud.

16. Put the container of hot oil/water in the fridge overnight and allow the oil to rise to the top.

17. The water that was added during the process catches all the extra plant material and brown carcinogens from the mixture. This allows for a much cleaner tasting product.

18. Pop the hardened green coconut oil off the top of the water that sunk to the bottom, and discard of the water.

19. You are now left with a green chunk of coconut oil that is ready to use for the recipe of your liking.

20. Store in the fridge until ready to use. Allow to warm before adding to recipes.

Pro Tip: Coconut oil is a good substitute for most baking and can replace butter in many recipes and some people like to add it to a hot beverage for an easy medication.

Cannabis infused coconut oil: The short method

Ingredients:

- Organic unrefined Coconut Oil

- 1 Ounce or less of dried and decarbed cannabis

Tools:

- Spatula

- Double boilers or au-Bain Marie

-- Fine Metal Strainer

- Bowl or jar with a lid that fits with the metal strainer

- jar with lid for storage

- Coffee grinder

- Cheese Cloth

Procedure:

1. Grind up your bud but don't get as fine as possible, just broken up in smaller pieces will do perfectly.

Note: it is important that you are using an ounce or less of bud because the time of the cooking process would take a lot longer if you use more, because there is more product to be infused and I would recommend using the long method.

2. Make sure it is decarbed before or after the grinding process by putting it on a dinner plate on a baking sheet in the oven for about an hour on 220F

3. The ratio I'd like to use is 1:10 so 1 ounce of weed on ten ounces of butter, so put your double boiler on the stove, low heat, and add the coconut oil.

4. Stir until your oil is fully melted, stirring helps the coconut oil to melt a little faster.

5. Add your decarbed bud and stir again until your bud is fully covered.

6. Let is simmer on low heat just keeping it around boiling point, 220F should be perfect.

7. Stir occasionally every 5 to 10 minutes for about 1 to 2 hours.

Note: The oil will turn really dark and your bud will almost look burned with a slight smell of buttered popcorn and coconut oil to it, but don't worry that is part of the process.

9. After 1-2 hours turn off the heat and let it cool down, no need to rush this process.

10. After your product cooled down, you can either choose to take out the top pot from the double boiler with your oil in it and put it in de freezer for two hours before straining it, adding more potency to your infusion or strain when it is cooled of and leave it in the fridge overnight.

11. Strain your oil by putting your steel strainer on a fitting bowl or jar, put the cheesecloth in your strainer, and slowly pour your oil and bud through the strainer.

12. If you used a jar with a lid you're finished to store, keep it cool in the fridge or in the freezer, I personally prefer the latter

13. Pour it from the bowl into your jar and store it.

Pro tip: Use the oil while it is cooled off but still liquid directly in your recipe, works perfectly with cake, cookies and brownies and makes the mixing process a lot easier! Make sure that it is cooled off as hot oil can burn or damage a plastic mixing bowl if you don't have a ceramic one.

Cannabis flour

This is one of the easiest ways to infuse your flour with cannabis; this can be useful for a vast array of different recipes for edibles and cannabis infusion in your favourite recipes.

It's easy and fast to make so it's always a good idea to have a batch on hand for future kitchen adventures.

Ingredients:

- ½ cup of finely ground bone-dry and decarbed marijuana for every 1 cup of flour.

Tools:

- Coffee grinder, your own cannabis grinder or a pestle and mortar

Procedure:

1. Ensure you have picked out every stem and seed from your marijuana

2. Ensure the marijuana is bone-dry and decarbed, to prevent mould growth during storage

3. Grind the marijuana as finely as possible

4. Mix with flour

5. Store in a cool, dark, dry place

Pro tip: Add a small amount of lecithin powder to your CannaFlour to help with the THC and CBD absorption for efficient and extra potent edibles.

Cannabis Milk

This is another easy way to consume or infuse weed into your recipes by making yourself some delicious Canna Milk or also called Marijuana Milk. Use this easy recipe and have a tea with milk that will really get you high or infuse anything that needs milk as an ingredient to make some potent edibles.

Ingredients:

- 1 pack of full fat milk *(you can use almond or coconut milk for a vegan alternative)*

- Ounce of finely powdered cannabis

Pro tip: A good rule of thumb is a joint worth of cannabis for each ¼ liter of milk. The more milk you use, the more cannabis you add proportionally.

Tools:

- 2 Cooking Pots for double boiler method, or 1 pot for the experts

- 1 Spatula

Procedure:

1. Bring your milk to boil and let simmer using the double boiler method, or if you're brave enough, direct low flame.

2. Add your cannabis to the milk bit by bit while stirring continuously, until the cannabis is completely covered by the milk.

3. Simmer and stir occasionally for 30-45 minutes.

4. You will start to notice that your milk will get a yellowish-green color.

5. Remove from the flame and strain well with a cheesecloth, making sure to squeeze out every last drop of green milk.

6. Allow it to cool and serve in shot glasses either warm or chilled.

7. For short time storage you can put this in the fridge; make sure it is airtight sealed and safe from spilling. Consume within two days.

8. For long time storage it would be best to store it frozen in a can or a jar that is airtight and properly sealed.

Important Note: If you notice skin forming on top of the milk, don't panic; just make sure to break it up by stirring!

Cannabis Infused Edible Recipes

Next up will be the recipes for some of the most classic and famous American dishes and snacks, be aware that creativity is key and where ever cannabutter is listed, you could potential switch out for the same amount of cannabis infused coconut oil, and a quick tip; everything that requires butter in or one of the listed sauces could potentially be infused, I always like to discover new ways to infuse tasty recipes and get creative with my cannabutter!

Main Course

Nacho's and pulled pork make up for the main course of this book, two easy to cook recipes that could be part of your dinner or as get baked lunch. We'll even dive into dips, sauces and soups in chapters afterwards but first these two. Southern style Barbeque has definitely a special place in my heart and this pulled pork recipe could also be done with a good piece of brisket by adding a few steps to the procedure. Creativity is key when it comes to cooking and everything you can do with regular butter, oils, flower, milk and more can be infused.

High noon Nacho's

Big fan of nachos, bigger fan of cannabis, these with paired with each other brings a little magic and the caution to watch the amount you're stuffing into your face! The munchies might be to be powerful but edibles can get uncomfortable, and you don't want a Mexican standoff between having the munchies and eating more edibles. Besides that, you could make those with indica strains cannabis butter and enjoy yourself some movies or have it the sativa way and invite some friends over.

Ingredients:

- 1 large sweet onion

- 1 green tomato

- 2 red tomatoes

- 1 jalapeno or Serrano pepper

- 2 cloves garlic, minced

- 3 tablespoons beer (a light beer like Corona is perfect)

- 3 tablespoons fresh lemon juice

- 3 tablespoons clarified cannabutter

- 6 ounces tortilla chips

- 1 cup shredded Tex Mex cheese

- 1 ripe avocado, diced

Tools:

- Blender or food processor

- Baking papers or cooking spray

- Baking Plate

Procedure:

1. Preheat oven to 350°F.

2. Roughly chop tomatoes, jalapeno, and onion. Add them to a blender (or food processor) with the garlic, beer, lemon juice and clarified cannabutter.

3. Pulse 3 times so that the texture becomes chunky.

4. Spread the chips on a baking plate covered with baking paper or cooking spray, cover with Tex Mex cheese.

5. Top the nacho's with several heaping spoonful's of the mixture you just made.

6. put it the baking sheet in the oven for 5 to 10 minutes (until you see that the cheese has melted).

7. Serve, topped with the avocado.

Pro-tip: Add more cheese, add blue cheese, add all the cheese and let it grill!

Infused Pulled Pork Sandwich

Barbecues every day! That is what I preach! Southern kitchen is definitely one of my favourites and maybe in the future I'll dedicate a whole book to infusing the Southern Kitchen for some really high barbecue cuisine!

Ingredients:

- 2 cups hickory wood chips

- 1 bone-in pork butt (7-9 lh), Boston butt or end-cut pork shoulder roast

- 1 tablespoon clarified Cannabutter

- 1 teaspoon kosher salt

- 1 teaspoon pepper

- 10 plain white hamburger buns (no sesame seeds), split

- Barbecue Sauce

- Coleslaw for serving

Tools:

- Medium sized bowl

- Charcoal or gas grill

- Brush

- Drip pan

Procedure:

1. Place wood chips in a medium bowl, cover with water. Soak for 30 minutes.

2. Brush pork with your clarified cannabutter, sprinkle with salt and pepper.

3. Use a charcoal or gas grill. For a charcoal grill, heat coals in center of grill to medium-low heat. Divide coals, placing half on each side of the grill, leaving center open. Place drip pan between coals. For gas grill, light two outside sections, leaving middle section unlit (three-burner grill). Or light one side and leave other side unlit (two-burner grill). Place drip pan on unlit side. Heat on high until hot.

4. Add wet wood chips to coals or place in smoking box of gas grill. (Or place chips in heavy-duty foil; fold to make packet. Poke holes in packet; place over indirect heat.)

5. Place pork, fat side up over drip pan. Grill, covered, over medium-low heat or coal 4-5 hours or until internal temperature reaches 190 or 200 degrees; adjusting heat or adding coals as necessary to maintain grill temperature of 325-350 degrees. Meat should be tender and falling apart, and bone should come out smooth and clean with no meat clinging to it. (This is the real test for doneness on the barbecue circuit.)

6. Let stand 20 minutes or until cool enough to handle. Remove skin, bones and fat. Reserve crisp edges; shred meat with two forks or chop with large knife. Chop

reserved crispy bits; add to pork. Stir in about 3/4 cup barbecue sauce or enough to moisten.

7. Serve in bun topped with some coleslaw.

8. Serve additional sauce on the side.

Pro tip: do this with brisket, but you'll need to sear it first before you put it on to the grill, supercharge it by using more cannabutter!

Cannaroni and Cheese

Only two main courses?! I couldn't leave this one out, this one is for you, definitely THE classic out there and it is making me hungry right now!

Ingredients:

- 8 ounces small elbow macaroni (about 2 cups)
- 1 teaspoon vegetable oil
- ¼ cup (1⁄2 stick) butter
- 8 teaspoons cannabutter
- 1 tablespoon all-purpose our 1 cup milk
- 1 cup half-and-half
- ½ teaspoon salt (kosher or sea) Pinch of freshly ground pepper
- 2 ¼ cups good-quality medium- sharp freshly shredded cheddar cheese, divided
- ½ cup cheddar crackers, crushed
- ½ cup bread crumbs

Tools:

- Large cooking pot
- Large strainer for the macaroni
- Large sauce pan
- Spatula
- Small sized bowl

Procedure:

1. Preheat the oven to 340°F and bring a large pot of salted water to a boil for the macaroni.

2. Cook the macaroni al dente, according to package directions.

3. Drain the macaroni and rinse it with cold water. Return it to the pot off the heat, toss it with the vegetable oil, and set it aside.

4. In a large saucepan, melt the butter and cannabutter over medium- low heat. Whisk in the flour, then whisk in the milk, half-and-half, salt, and pepper. Cook, stirring until the mixture thickens enough to coat the back of a spoon, 3 to 4 minutes.

5. Stir in 2 cups of the cheddar and mix well.

6. Add the cooked pasta to the cheese mixture, mixing thoroughly.

7. Turn the mixture into a buttered 9-by-13-inch casserole dish.

8. In a small bowl, combine the remaining 1/4 cup cheddar, cheddar crackers, and bread crumbs and sprinkle the mixture evenly on top of the pasta.

9. Bake until the topping is golden brown in approximately 30 to 40 minutes.

Pro tip: add pepperoni sausage, chorizo and bacon in small pieces on top of that cheese before it goes in to the oven. Also perfect to mix into your macaroni!

Dips and sauces

"Drizzle that sauce, Boss!", and dip your finger food into one of these amazing infused dips and sauces. From a real banger such as BHO infused BBQ sauce to cannamel infused sauce for the sweet tooth, this will have you covered with your kitchen dripping, dipping and drizzling essentials for medication.

High Noon Salsa

This can be your go to dip for all your baguettes, pains and nacho's, or just stuff it in your quesadilla or burrito.

Ingredients:

- 2 cups fresh tomatoes, chopped
- ½ cup green bell pepper, diced
- ½ cup onion, diced
- ¼ cup Cannabutter
- 1 tablespoons fresh cilantro, diced
- 1 tablespoon
- ½ fresh jalapeno, diced with seeds
- Salt and pepper to taste
- Fresh lime juice to taste

Tools:

- Medium sized mixing bowl
- Food processor

Procedure:

1. Toss all ingredients after u finished cutting them together in a medium sized mixing bowl.

2. Toss the containments of your bowl into your food processor and pulse three times until it becomes chunky

3. Serve immediately or chill in the refrigerator.

Cannabis infused BBQ sauce

BBQ sauce goes with a lot of things especially grilled and slow cooked meat. My favourite way of using this is to dissolve a gram of Rosin tested at 70% in the cannabutter and coconut oil mixture and let it simmer at a low temperature for about an hour with a knife point of lecithin added after you cool your mixture down to add a whopping 700 mg of THC to end product and use it to caramelize bacon strips. Ideally you want the measure out the sauce to get about 10 to 40 THC mg per bacon strip; for 40 mg THC per strip you would need about 15 pieces of bacon. Put those rubbed in with all that BBQ goodness in the oven at about 400F for 5-8 minutes. If you dissolved the BHO well enough the THC will bind itself to fat so make sure to not spill any of that bacon grease and drizzle it over afterwards, also watch out that you're not using a crazy amount of grease as this will be quite potent.

Ingredients:

- ½ tablespoon of very potent cannabutter

- ½ tbsp. of very potent coconut oil

- 2 cups ketchup

- 1 cup dark brown sugar

- 1/4cup molasses

- 1/4cup apple cider vinegar

- ½ cup organic apple juice

- 2 tablespoons Worcestershire sauce

- 1/4 cup Dijon mustard

- 2 tablespoons paprika

- 2 tablespoons black pepper

- 1 tablespoon Cayenne pepper

  2 tablespoons garlic salt

- 3 tablespoons liquid smoke

- 1/8 cup cold water mixed with

- 1 tablespoon corn-starch (optional for a thicker sauce)

Tools:

- Small sauce pan

- Spatula

- Medium size cooking pot

- Whisk

Procedure:

1. First, melt your cannabutter and infused coconut oil in a small saucepan stir this until its fully liquid for about 5 minutes, then set aside.

2. Combine the ketchup, brown sugar, molasses, apple cider vinegar, apple juice, Worcestershire, mustard, in a medium size sauce pot and stir. Add the paprika, pepper, salt and liquid smoke and whisk.

3. Bring to a boil, and then reduce heat to low and simmer for 30 minutes. Add the corn-starch mixture along with the cannabis infused butter mixture and simmer another 5 to 10 minutes, stirring frequently, until desired thickness is reached.

Pro tip: Throw a gram of BHO with 70% THC in your butter and coconut infusion and let it simmer until it is dissolved to add a whopping 700 mg of THC to your sauce, be very careful and calculated with dosing because this will you with a ten ton hammer!

Mary Jane's Pizza Sauce

Pizzas are essential to life, pizza is life, cannabis and pizza is a match made in heaven, and generally things tend to get a lot better when pizza is involved but add some cannabis and your pizza turns into medicine magic. Infusing your sauce is the way to go on this one, as cannabis infused pizza sauce gives you the freedom to get creative with this one!

Ingredients:

- 1 can tomato paste (6 oz.)

- 1 cup water

- ½ cup Cannabutter

- 2 cloves garlic, minced

- ½ tablespoon dried basil

- ½ tablespoon dried oregano

- ½ tablespoon dried rosemary

- ½ teaspoon salt

- ½ teaspoon black pepper

Tools:

- Small sauce pan

- Spatula

Procedure:

1. Mix all ingredients in small saucepan and stir well.

2. Bring mixture to a light boil.

3. Turn heat to low and simmer for 30 minutes. Stir occasionally.

4. Remove pan from heat, let cool.

5. Transfer cooled sauce to Mason jar and cover.

6. Chill sauce in refrigerator for 2 hours before serving for best flavour. Shake occasionally.

7. Make some Marijuana Pizza!

Pro tip: you could use BBQ sauce for your pizza too, and if you like bacon, pepperoni, salami, chorizo, chicken or other meat on your pizza you should definitely try it out.

Infused Spaghetti Sauce

The classic spaghetti sauce; one of my first introductions to cannabis infused cooking, to be honest I didn't even notice it back then because we were totally baked; smoking blunts and blazing like chimneys before we got to dinner. Definitely a must do if you're having friends over for a dinner and a birthday party!

Ingredients:

- 1 can (26 oz.) crushed tomatoes

- 1 can (26 oz.) tomato puree

- 1 can (26 oz.) tomato sauce

- 2 teaspoons of very potent clarified cannabutter

- 1 large green pepper, chopped

- 1 large white onion, chopped

- 1 cup fresh mushrooms, sliced

- 1 tablespoon oregano

- 1 tablespoon parsley

- 1 can (8 oz.) tomato paste

- 2 cloves garlic, finely chopped

- 1 teaspoon garlic powder

- 2 teaspoon onion powder

- salt to taste

- sugar to taste

Tools:

-Large stock pot

-Medium sized frying pan

Procedure:

1. In a large stock pot, stir together crushed tomatoes, tomato puree and tomato sauce. Set on medium-low heat and cover.

2. Meanwhile in a medium sized pan, heat some clarified cannabutter over medium heat. When this is warm, add peppers, onions and mushrooms.

3. Sprinkle with a dash of salt and pepper to taste. Sauté until onions are clear but not browned. Add sautéed vegetables with the butter to your stock pot, folding them into the sauce with the oregano and parsley. Cover and bring to a slow simmer, stirring occasionally from the bottom up.

4. Once simmering add the tomato paste, fresh garlic, garlic powder and onion powder. Make sure to mix thoroughly. Turn to low heat and simmer, covered at least 1 hour.

6. Taste, if too acidy add sugar 1/2 teaspoon at a time, checking every 10 minutes.

7. After you tasted it for about 6 times, take the sauce off your stove after it simmered for about an hour and let it cool off

8. Keep refrigerated for storage, you could also freeze it for long term storage.

Note: You might get high if you taste too much. Be careful if that is not what you want.

Pro tip: add a tablespoon of kief just before you let it simmer for an hour, this will help in the process of decarbing your kief or you could decarb it before you add it to the sauce.

High Noon Guacamole

Guacamole is super healthy and it basically goes on everything especially my sandwiches. Also great with nacho's.

Ingredients:

- 2 large ripe avocados, peeled and seeded

- Juice of 2 medium limes

- 4 teaspoons of clarified cannabutter

- ½ small red onion, diced

- ¼ cup finely chopped cilantro leaves

- ½ teaspoon kosher salt

- 1 small tomato, seeded and chopped (optional)

Tools:

- Medium sized bowl

- Spatula, whisk or mixer

Procedure:

1. In a medium bowl, mash the avocado.

2. Add all the other ingredients and mix thoroughly.

Note: To keep your guacamole from turning brown, drizzle some citrus juice on that guac and press plastic wrap snugly into its surface (this limits the oxygen exposure that leads to browning).

Pro tip: Add jalapeno peppers and a table spoon of black pepper for that extra kick!

Kush berry Sauce

Great with ice-cream and all the other sweet dessert and breakfast recipes, I'd recommend sativa strains in your sauce in the morning, because a wake and bake with indica is your ticket back to bed.

Ingredients:

- 1 pound strawberries, hulled and finely chopped

- 1/4 cup honey

- 2 tablespoons clarified cannabutter

- 1/2 cup freshly squeezed orange juice (from 2 medium oranges)

- 2 teaspoons corn-starch Pinch of salt (kosher or sea)

Tools:

- Small sauce pan

- Small Bowl

- Spatula or whisk

- Spoon

Procedure:

1. In a small saucepan, combine the strawberries, honey, and clarified cannabutter and heat over medium-low heat.

2. In a small bowl, combine the orange juice with the corn-starch.

3. Add the corn-starch mixture to the berries and stir until the sauce begins to thicken and coats the back of a spoon, about 8-10 minutes.

4. Remove from heat. (The sauce will continue to thicken as it cools.)

5. Stir in the salt.

High Noon Nacho Cheese

Ingredients:

- ½ cup clarified cannabutter

- 12 ounces 4-cheese, shredded

- 10 ounces canned diced tomatoes

- 8 ounces sharp cheddar cheese, shredded

- 2 cups cannamilk

- 1 cup heavy cream

- ½ cup Parmesan cheese

- ½-⅔ cup hot sauce, make it as hot as you want

- ¼ cup flour

- 2 tablespoons goat cheese or cream cheese

- 2 tablespoons chipotle in adobo sauce

- 1 tablespoon garlic

- 1 tablespoon red chilli powder

- 1 pinch salt

Tools:

- Sauté pan

- Spatula

- Whisk

- Serving bowl

Procedure:

1. In a sauté pan over medium-high heat, simmer your clarified CannaButter for 45-60 seconds.

2. Add the garlic, chilli powder, and flour, and cook for 3-4 minutes.

3. Add cream cheese, and cook for 1-2 minutes, stirring constantly. Add milk and heavy cream, whisk and cook for an additional 2-3 minutes.

4. Add the Parmesan and your shredded 4-cheese blend, and whisk until all the cheeses are well combined.

5. Stir in the diced tomatoes, and chipotle, then whisk in your cheddar cheese until smooth.

6. Add the hot sauce and stir thoroughly.

7. Add the hot sauce and stir thoroughly.

8. Transfer your Nacho Cheese to a serving bowl, and enjoy!

Mary Jane's Magic Hummus

Ingredients:

- 1 tablespoon water

- 1 medium garlic clove, coarsely chopped

- ¼ cup tahini

- 1 tablespoon freshly squeezed lemon juice

- 1 (15-ounce) can chickpeas, drained and rinsed

- 2 tablespoons clarified cannabutter

- 1 teaspoon freshly grated lemon zest

- 1/4 teaspoon smoked sweet paprika 1/4 teaspoon ground turmeric

- Salt (kosher or sea) and freshly ground black pepper, to taste

Tools:

- Food processor

- serving bowl

Procedure:

1. In the bowl of a food processor fitted with a metal blade, pulse the water, garlic, tahini, and lemon juice to a smooth paste.

2. Add half of the chickpeas and pulse to combine. Scrape down the sides of the bowl before adding the remaining chickpeas.

3. With the machine running, add the clarified cannabutter in a steady stream through the feed tube. Blend until the hummus reaches your desired consistency.

4. Add the zest, paprika, turmeric, salt, and pepper and pulse briefly to combine.

5. Serve in a bowl for dipping.

Cannabis infused caramel sauce

Ingredients:

- 1 cup brown sugar, packed

- ½ cup granulated sugar

- ¾ cup heavy cream

- ½ cup CannaButter

- ½ cup water, distilled

- ½ teaspoon sea salt

- ½ tablespoon vanilla extract

Tools:

- Spatula

- Mason jar with lid

- Medium-sized saucepan

Procedure:

1. Mix the brown sugar, granulated sugar, heavy cream, CannaButter, water and salt together in saucepan over medium heat.

2. Whisk constantly and gently for 8 minutes, or until sauce starts to thicken. Be careful not to burn. Adjust heat as necessary.

3. Stir in the vanilla extract and heat for an additional minute.

4. Turn off stove and remove pan from the heat. Allow sauce to cool for 5 minutes.

5. Transfer caramel sauce to Mason jar. Use spatula to scrape all sauce from the pan.

6. Refrigerate until cold. Keep in the refrigerator.

Cannabis infused Soups

The best idea for when it gets colder, I must honestly say I don't make these very often; I tried it out but when it comes to cooking cannabis I tend to keep to the small, quick and fast edibles, but this is definitely your go-to when you want to surprise your guests with a 3 course 420 dinner. Let me tell you that you probably should inform before them unless it is your cranky, nagging mother-in-law, she might need to chill out a little. But seriously always let people know what they're getting themselves into because education is the key for a good experience.

Extra Green Broccoli Soup

Broccoli is one my favourite veggies, especially with chicken and rice. Now this soup even adds a little of that green punch to gently knock you off your socks. A must try if you want to go all out cannabis cuisine!

Ingredients:

- 4 tablespoons cannabutter

- 1 small onion, chopped

- 3 tablespoons all-purpose flour

- 2 cups vegetable stock

- 1 large head broccoli, cut into florets

- 2 cups of milk

- 1 cup half-and-half milk

- 3 cups freshly shredded cheddar cheese, plus extra for garnish

- Salt (kosher or sea) and freshly ground black pepper, to taste

Tools:

- Large cooking pot

- Spatula

- Wooden spoon

- Food Processor or immersion blender

Procedure:

1. In a large cooking pot, melt the cannabutter over medium-low heat.

2. Add the onion and sauté the onions until gold brown, 4 to 5 minutes.

3. Sprinkle in the flour and cook, stirring, for 1 to 2 minutes to eliminate the raw flour taste, not letting it brown.

4. Add the stock and broccoli and cook for 9 minutes, Turn off the heat and let the soup cool slightly.

5. Try working in 2 batches; puree the soup in a blender or food processor. Or, if you have an immersion blender, you can puree the soup directly in the pot.

6. Return the blended soup to the pot. Over medium-low heat, add the milk, half-and-half, and cheddar, and stir until cheese melts.

7. Season the soup with salt and pepper, and garnish with more cheddar before serving.

Mary Jane's Tomato Soup

Another classic you can't miss.

Ingredients:

- 2 tablespoons clarified cannabutter

- 1 medium onion, chopped

- 1-quart vegetable or chicken stock

- 1 (28-ounce) can of crushed tomatoes

- 1 cup half-and-half milk

- Salt (kosher or sea) and freshly ground black pepper, to taste

- 8 leaves chopped fresh basil or 2 chopped scallions for garnish

- 4 tablespoons shredded mozzarella

Tools:

- Medium cooking pot

- Food processor or Immersion blender

Procedure:

1. In a medium pot, heat the cannabutter over medium heat. Add the onions and sauté until golden brown, 6 to 7 minutes.

2. Add the stock and tomatoes and cook until they are warmed through. Add the half-and-half milk and season the soup with salt and pepper.

3. Simmer the soup, stirring occasionally, until it has heated through, 15 to 20 minutes. Turn on the heat and let the soup cool slightly.

4. Try to work in 2 batches, puree the soup in a blender or food processor. Or, if you have an immersion blender, you can puree the soup directly in the pot.

5. Return the blended soup to the pot and rewarm it over medium-low heat.

6. Garnish with the basil or scallions and mozzarella before serving.

Cannabis Infused Sweet Potato Soup

Ingredients:

- 3 large sweet potatoes, peeled and cut in sections

- 2-3 tablespoons clarified cannabutter

- 3 scallions, chopped

- 3 strips bacon, cooked until crisp, drained of grease and chopped

- 2 teaspoons chilli powder

- ½ teaspoon cayenne powder

- ½ teaspoon salt

- 2 tablespoons half and half

- 3-4 cups stock, chicken or vegetable

Tools:

- Large Soup pot

- Medium sauce pan

- Spatula

- Wooden Spoon

- Food processor

Procedure:

1. Place the potatoes in a large soup pot and cover with water by several inches. Simmer the sweet potato till very tender, about 20-25 minutes. Drain.

2. While the potatoes are cooking, heat a medium saucepan with the cannabutter.

3. Sauté the scallions for 3-4 minutes, stirring occasionally. Add the bacon to the pan and stir to absorb the canna-butter.

4. In a small bowl combine the scalllon and bacon and set aside.

5. Place the cooked sweet potato in the bowl of your food processor and puree.

6. Gradually add the remaining ingredients, ending with the stock, until completely smooth.

7. Heat the soup before serving.

8. Ladle into serving bowls and top with the scallion bacon garnish.

Pro-tip: Serve with bread for dipping pleasure.

Sweets and Desserts

This is my collection of some amazing recipes for the sweet tooth, I am a cookies man myself but I definitely tried all them out as they are just too delicious to pass by. From your American cuisine classics such as Wake and Bake Pancakes or The Chocolate Canna-banana split to Cherry Pie, candy and sweets. I'd recommend every single one of them as my favourite but it's up to you.

Cannabis Chocolate Sauce

I never made a chocolate sauce I didn't like except for this one time where I was already really baked on some edibles and I let my chocolate sauce burn by forgetting all about it, Luckily I didn't put in my cannabutter yet but sad things already happened. With this recipe for cannabis infused chocolate sauce you can easily make yourself some chocolate sauce covered ice cream or just pair with anything that needs a little of that special sauce.

Ingredients:

- 1 cup heavy cream
- 2 tablespoons cannabutter
- 8 ounces dark chocolate, finely chopped

Tools:

- 2 Cooking pots for the double boiler method
- 1 Spatula

Procedure:

1. In a double boiler or heat-proof bowl set over set over just-simmering water, heat the cream and cannabutter, stirring occasionally to be sure the butter has melted.

2. When the butter has completely melted, add the chocolate. Stir until the chocolate has completely melted and the mixture is smooth.

3. Chocolate can be stored in the fridge for a long time, for use just heat it up using the double boiler method.

Chocolate Canna-Banana Split

One of my favourite desserts made perfect with some Cannabis infused Chocolate sauce. Superfast and easy to make if you already got some cannabis chocolate sauce in storage and you need to make some quick dessert.

Ingredients:

- 1 banana, peeled, cut lengthways

- 3 scoops vanilla ice-cream

- Chopped nuts

- Cannabis Chocolate sauce

- Whipped cream

Tools:

- 1 Knife

- Plates

Procedure:

1. Place your banana slices on a plate. Top with scoops of ice-cream. Drizzle with cannabis-infused chocolate sauce. Squirt the cream and sprinkle the nuts. Serve your delicious Banana Split!

Pro tip: Add Nutella, things in life always get better with a swirl of Nutella drizzled on those bananas.

Cannabis Doughnuts

Cannabis Infused Doughnuts is definitely one of my favourite recipes for a sweet tooth cheat-day wake and bake!

Ingredients:

- ¼ cup CannaFlour

- ¼ cup pastry flour

- 1 teaspoon baking powder

- ½ cup sugar

- 1 teaspoon cinnamon

- ½ tsp. salt

- 3 tablespoons butter

- ½ cup CannaMilk

- 1 teaspoon vanilla extract

- 1 egg, beaten

- ½ cup powdered sugar

Tools:

- 1 Bowl

- 1 Spatula

- Mini doughnut pan, greased

Procedure:

1. Preheat the oven to 350 degrees.

2. Cream together the butter and the sugar.

3. Add the cannamilk, vanilla extract and egg. Stir until combined.

3. Mix in the CannaFlour, pastry flour and baking powder.

4. Add cinnamon and salt. Mix well.

5. Spoon mixture into mini doughnut pan, filling each doughnut cup about ¾ full.

6. Bake doughnuts in preheated oven until doughnuts are a light golden brown. Usually 5 to 9 minutes. Watch closely.

7. Let doughnuts cool for 5 minutes before removing from pan.

8. Roll each doughnut in powdered sugar

Pro tip: You could potentially switch out the regular butter with some cannabutter and drizzle some of that cannabis infused chocolate sauce on top, but beware as those doughnuts will become extremely potent and not comfortable for someone with a low tolerance for THC!

Cannabis Infused Cherry Pie

Ingredients:

- 2 sheets of refrigerated pie crusts
- 4 cups fresh cherries, pitted
- 1 cup sugar
- ½ cup CannaFlour
- ¼ cup CannaButter, melted
- ½ teaspoon vanilla extract
- 1 teaspoon sugar

Tools:

- 1 pie dish

- A pair of Kitchen Scissors

- 1 Bowl

- 1 spatula

- Oven

Procedure:

1. Press one pie crust sheet firmly into the bottom of the pie dish and up the sides of the pan.

2. Trim the edge of the dough with kitchen scissors; leave 1 inch of dough to hang over edge of pan. Set aside.

3. Stir together the cherries, sugar, CannaFlour, cannabutter, and vanilla extract.

4. Transfer the cherry filling mix to the dough-lined pie dish.

5. Place the second pie sheet over the filled pie. Trim edges appropriately, leaving 1 inch of dough hanging.

6. Fold the edge of the top layer of dough under the edge of the bottom layer of dough. Pinch dough sheets together to seal.

7. Cut 6 slits on the top of the dough to allow steam to escape.

8. Put the uncooked pie in the refrigerator to firm the dough (about 20 minutes).

9. Preheat oven to 375 degrees.

10. Remove pie from refrigerator and bake the pie in the preheated oven for 1 hour or until crust is golden brown and filling is bubbling.

11. Transfer pie to a wire rack and sprinkle with remaining teaspoon of sugar. Let cool to completely set for at least 1 hour before serving.

Cinnamon Roll Filling

This is necessary to make your perfect Cannabis Cinnamon Rolls.

Ingredients:

- ½ cup butter, softened

- ½ cup granulated sugar

  ¼ cup firmly packed brown sugar

- 6 tablespoons all-purpose flour

- 1 ½ tablespoons ground cinnamon

Tools:

- 1 Spatula

- 1 Bowl for mixing

Procedure:

1. Combine all ingredients, stirring until blended.

Pro Tip: you could use cannabutter to supercharge your cinnamon rolls but beware as this will be very potent because you're already using at least one of the cannabis infused ingredients for your recipe!

Cannabis Cinnamon Rolls

One for your perfect wake and bake, an American classic so be sure to try this one out!

Ingredients:

- Dough

- 3 cups CannaFlour

- 3 tablespoons sugar

- 1 teaspoon salt

- 2 teaspoons yeast

- ½ cup CannaMilk

- 3 tablespoons butter, melted

- 1 egg

- Cinnamon Roll Filling

- ¼ cup CannaButter, softened

- ½ cup brown sugar, packed

- 2 tablespoons cinnamon

- Glaze

- ¼ cup Cannabis Cream Cheese, room temperature

- 1 cup powdered sugar

- ¼ cup CannaButter, melted

- ½ teaspoon vanilla extract

- Oil or butter for greasing

Tools:

- Mixing bowls

- Spatula

- Baking Pan

- Cooking oil

- Oven

- Aluminium Foil

Procedure:

1. Mix 2 1/2 cups of the CannaFlour, sugar, salt, and yeast together in a large bowl. Set aside.

2. In a separate bowl, combine the CannaMilk and melted butter together. Add the milk mixture to the flour mixture and stir to combine.

3. Add the egg to the mixture. Begin mixing in the remaining 1/2 cup of the CannaFlour, only enough to make soft dough. Mix everything together.

4. Knead the dough for 5 minutes on a lightly floured surface.

5. Set kneaded dough aside in a lightly greased bowl for 15 minutes.

6. Roll the dough out on the floured surface. Shape the dough into a rectangle (about 9"x13").

7. Prepare the filling by spreading 1/4 cup of softened CannaButter on top of the dough.

8. Sprinkle brown sugar and cinnamon on top of the dough.

9. Roll the dough length-wise into a spiralled log shape.

10. Slice the dough evenly into 10-12 pieces and place in greased 9-inch round pan.

11. Cover the baking pan and dough with aluminium foil and allow dough to rise for 1 hour. Rolls will be ready to bake once the dough has doubled in size.

12. Preheat the oven to 375 degrees.

13. Bake dough for 20-25 minutes in preheated oven, or until lightly browned.

14. In the last 5 minutes of baking, begin making the glaze. Mix the Cannabis Cream Cheese, powdered sugar, melted CannaButter and vanilla extract together. Mix vigorously until smooth.

15. Remove cooked cinnamon rolls from the oven. Immediately spread glaze on top and serve hot.

Wake and Bake Pancakes

Everyone knows that pancakes are awesome. Guess what, Wake and Bake cannabis Infused pancakes are even better. Pancakes are super easy to make and with this special wake and bake recipe you'll have the best breakfast and medication at the same time!

Ingredients:

- 3 ½ tablespoons Cannabutter

- 1 ½ cups CannaFlour

- 3 tablespoons Sugar

- 1 ½ teaspoon Baking powder

- ½ teaspoon salt

- 1 ½ cups CannaMilk

- ½ tablespoon vanilla or vanilla sugar

- 2 large eggs

Tools:

- 2 medium sized Mixing bowls

- Spatula

- Frying Pan

- Cooking oil

Procedure:

1. Take one bowl and mix together the flour, baking powder, sugar and salt.

2. Mix the milk, eggs, the melted weed butter and the vanilla in a separate bowl.

3. Now combine both mixes into a pancake batter. When you mix the content of the two bowls together, it's best when you keep the batter somewhat lumpy. This way, your pancakes will turn out nice and fluffy. At this point, you can also add some other goodies to the batter, like nuts, fruits, berries, chocolate chips…

4. On your stove, put a frying pan with some oil and set it on medium heat.

5. When the oil has reached temperature, pour about 1/4 cup of your batter for each pancake onto the frying pan.

6. The pancakes are ready to flip when you see bubbles appear on top. With a spatula, flip them over and cook them on the other side. Your pancakes are ready when they're golden brown.

7. Serve them right away with maple syrup, sugar or however you like them!

Pro tip: Nutella, Ice-cream and some of that Cannabis Chocolate sauce drizzled on top make up for the best Wake and Bake pancakes ever!

Jolly Jane Ranchers

Hard candy or cannabis infused candy, simple choice as I like to keep my diet clean so all my little sins are strictly edibles, They help me get through my day and relieve my pain in a candy form is just a win-win situation for me!

Ingredients:

- A big bag of Jolly Ranchers.

  Cannabis tincture

- ¼ cup water

Tools:

- Candy Thermometer

- Ceramic Cooking Pot

- Coffee Grinder

- Candy molds (optional)

Procedure:

1. Grind up the Jolly Ranchers in a coffee grinder. Use all the same colors if you want to have a specific color. If not, throw them all in!

2. Put ground Jolly Ranchers and water into a pot on a stove and bring the temperature to 300 degrees exactly using candy thermometer

3. Once 300 degrees is reached, take off heat and add as much tincture as you want

4. Pour the contents into candy molds, or onto a cookie sheet covered in non-stick foil, and let it harden

5. Don't eat them when they're too hot and enjoy!

Mary-Jane's Strawberries

Ingredients:

- 1 ½ cups white chocolate chips

- ¼ cup Cannabis Coconut Oil

- 20 strawberries (with stems)

- ¼ cup blue sprinkles

Tools:

- Microwave safe bowl

- Wax lined Plate

Procedure:

1. Heat white chocolate and Cannabis Coconut Oil in a microwave safe bowl. Remove and stir every 20 seconds until melted.

2. Dip dry strawberries in chocolate one at a time, allowing excess chocolate to drip back into bowl.

3. Dip the tips of each chocolate coated strawberry into the blue sprinkles.

4. Sit strawberries on wax lined plate to dry.

5. Chill strawberries in fridge 20 minutes before serving.

Chocolate Chip Cookies

The classic that every cannabis enthusiast has to try at least once. My all-time favorite easy to bake medible, as I said before I am a cookies man and this one is my go to recipe for the lazy days. I don't recommend using CannaFlour in your cookies unless you don't mind the intense green taste you will get.

Ingredients:

- 1 cup Cannabutter, softened

- 1 cup white sugar

- 1 cup packed brown sugar

- 2 eggs

- 2 teaspoon vanilla extract

- 3 cups all-purpose flour

- 1 teaspoon baking soda

- 2 teaspoons hot water

- ½ teaspoon salt

- 2 cups semisweet chocolate chips

- 1 cup chopped walnuts

Tools:

- Electric Mixer or whisk

- Medium Sized Bowl for mixing

- Baking Paper

Procedure:

1. Preheat oven to 350°F (175°C).

2. Cream together the Cannabutter, white sugar, and brown sugar until it is smooth. Beat in the eggs one at a time and then stir in the vanilla in your medium sized bowl. Dissolve baking soda in hot water. Add to batter along with salt. Stir in flour, chocolate chips, and nuts.

3. Drop large spoon fulls of your cookie dough from the bowl onto baking plate covered with baking paper.

4. Bake for about 10 minutes in the preheated oven or until edges are nicely browned.

5. Remove the cookies from the oven and let them cool on the baking papers for 2 minutes. Transfer the cookies to a wire rack to cool completely.

6. Repeat with the remaining dough, cooling the baking sheets between batches.

7. Store cookies in an airtight container.

Chocolate Infused Espresso Cookies

These cookies would be the best with a sativa strain for your daily medication; great for fulfilling your daily tasks so try these out for your wake and bake!

Ingredients:

- 2 cups all-purpose flour

- 2/3 cup unsweetened cocoa powder

- 2 teaspoons instant espresso powder

- 1 teaspoon baking soda

- ¼ teaspoon salt (kosher or sea)

- 1/2 cup (1 stick) unsalted butter, softened

- ½ cup (8 tablespoons) clarified cannabutter, softened

- 1 cup granulated sugar

- ½ cup packed brown sugar

- 2 eggs

- 2 teaspoons vanilla extract

- 1 cup bittersweet chocolate chips

- 2/3 cup white chocolate chips

Tools:

- Electric stand or hand Mixer

- Whisk

- Medium Sized Bowl for mixing

- Baking Paper

Procedure:

1. Preheat the oven to 340°F.

2. In a medium bowl, whisk together the flour, cocoa and espresso powders, baking soda, and salt.

3. In the bowl of a stand mixer fitted with the paddle attachment (or use an electric hand mixer or a wooden spoon in a large bowl), combine the unsalted butter, cannabutter, granulated sugar, and brown sugar. Beat on medium speed until fluffy.

3. Reduce the speed to low and add the eggs and vanilla. Beat until well mixed, about 1 minute.

4. Add the flour mixture and mix until just combined. Stir in the bittersweet and white chocolate chips.

5. Drop the dough by heaping tablespoons onto the prepared baking sheets, about 2 inches apart.

6. Bake until the cookies are set and no longer shiny, 7 to 9 minutes.

7. Remove the cookies from the oven and let them cool on the baking papers for 2 minutes. Transfer the cookies to a wire rack to cool completely.

8. Repeat with the remaining dough, cooling the baking sheets between batches.

9. Store cookies in an airtight container.

Pro tip: Cookies dipped in cannamilk.

Cannapple Pie

Cannabis infused Classic Apple Pie, enough said.

Ingredients:

- 2 sheets of refrigerated pie crusts
- 6 cups apples, cored, peeled, and sliced (Granny Smith, Golden Delicious or Honey Crisp)
- 1 tablespoon fresh lemon juice
- 1/3 cup brown sugar
- ½ cup granulated sugar
- 1 ½ cups CannaButter, cubed or clarified
- 1/8 cup flour
- 1 teaspoon ground cinnamon
- 1/8 teaspoon ground nutmeg
- ½ teaspoon salt

Tools:

- Pie dish or pan
- A pair of Kitchen Scissors
- Bowl
- Spatula

Procedure:

1. Press a pie crust sheet firmly into the bottom of a pie dish and up the sides of the pan.

2. Trim the edge of the dough with kitchen scissors, leaving 1 inch of dough to hang over the edge of the pan. Set aside.

3. Combine the apples and lemon juice in a large bowl, mix well.

4. Add brown sugar, granulated sugar, flour, cinnamon, salt and nutmeg. Mix well, making sure to coat all the apples.

5. Transfer the filling mix to the dough-lined pan.

6. Disperse cubed or clarified CannaButter on top of the apple filling evenly.

7. Place the second pie sheet over the filled pie. Trim edges appropriately, leaving 1 inch of dough hanging.

8. Fold the edge of the top layer of dough under the edge of the bottom layer of dough. Pinch dough sheets together to seal.

9. Cut an "X" across the top center of the dough to allow steam to escape, alternatively poke the dough with a fork.

10. Put the uncooked pie in the refrigerator for 20 minutes to firm the dough.

11. Preheat oven to 375 degrees.

12. Remove pie from refrigerator and bake for 1 hour or until crust is golden brown and the filling is bubbling.

13. Transfer the apple pie to a wire rack and let it cool for at least 1 hour before serving.

Pro tip: add whipped cream with serving!

Cannabanana-Peanut Butter Ice Cream

Best to serve cold while it is hot outside, be cautious, hot weather and medibles can turn you in to a sloth and too much will be quite uncomfortable.

Ingredients:

- 2 cups Almond or coconut Milk (½ of both is possible)

- 1 cup CannaMilk

- ½ cup sugar

- 1 tablespoon corn starch

- Pinch of salt

- 4 bananas, pureed

- ½ cup peanut butter (optional)

Tools:

- 1½ quart ice cream freezer container

- Large saucepan

- Fine strainer

- Large bowl

- Whisk

- Spatula

- Electric hand mixer

Procedure:

1. Combine CannaMilk, almond milk, coconut milk, sugar and corn-starch in a large saucepan and whisk together thoroughly. Cook over medium heat while stirring constantly until mixture starts to thicken, about 10 minutes. Remove from heat and allow to warm.

2. Pour the warm cannamilk mixture through a fine strainer and into a large bowl. Discard any solids.

3. Chill the cannamilk mixture uncovered in refrigerator for 1 hour; stir occasionally. Place plastic wrap on top of milk mixture after 1 hour. Let chill for another 12 to 24 hours.

4. Pour cold mixture into 1½ quart ice cream freezer container and freeze.

5. Remove container from freezer after 2 hours, or until ice cream starts to firm but is still soft. Stir in banana puree and peanut butter with your spatula.

6. Mix well until peanut butter is equally distributed.

7. Return the container to freezer for another 6 hours, or until ice cream is firm.

8. Let it stand at room temperature for 5 minutes before serving.

Pro tip: Drizzle some jelly on top of your ice-cream to get some of that Peanut Butter Jelly Cannabanana action going and enjoy this epic combination! For super charge: add some extra cannamilk; mix it up in to a milk shake and have all the boys chilling in your yard!

Mary's Berries Sherbet

Ingredients:

- 5 cups fresh blackberries

- 2 cups sugar

- 2 ½ cups CannaMilk

- 1 tablespoon lemon juice

Tools:

- Food Processor or Blender

- Strainer

- Medium sized bowl

- Ice cream freezer container

Procedure:

1. Blend blackberries and sugar together in food processor until smooth.

2. Pour the pureed berries through strainer and into a bowl. Discard seeds.

3. Mix the Cannamilk into the blackberry puree. Stir in lemon juice.

4. Pour berry/milk mixture into an ice cream freezer container; freeze for 3 hours.

5. Let stand at room temperature for 5 minutes before serving.

No Bake Fudge

Ingredients:

- 2 lbs. / 7 cups of powdered sugar

- 1 cup of cocoa powder

- 1 lb. (4 sticks) of cannabutter

- 1 tsp. of vanilla essence

- 1 cup of peanut butter

Tools:

- Saucepan or double boiler

- Large bowl

- Spatula or whisk

- Flat pan

Procedure:

1. Melt the butter and peanut butter in a saucepan or double boiler, and add the vanilla essence

2. In a large bowl, mix together the powdered sugar and cocoa.

3. Add the melted ingredients and mix well

4. Press into a flat pan, and place in the fridge until firm

Mary Jane's Snacks

Snack time, the best time, don't forget that you're cooking with pot so watch your munchies as you indulge in the amazing world of delicious cannabis infused snack recipes.

Cannabis Granola

Ingredients:

- 1 1/2 cups rolled oats

- 1/4 cup chopped walnuts

- 1/4 cup shredded unsweetened coconut

- 2 tablespoons dried chopped cherries

- 2 tablespoons whole flaxseed

- 2 tablespoons clarified cannabutter

- 2 tablespoons honey

- 1/2 teaspoon ground cinnamon

Tools:

- Large bowl
- Baking sheets

Procedure:

1. Preheat the oven to 300°F.

2. Put all the ingredients in a large bowl and toss together well. Taste and add more honey or cinnamon, if desired.

3. Spread the granola in one layer on a rimmed baking sheet.

4. Bake your granola, stirring every 10 minutes, until golden brown, about 30 minutes.

5. Let the granola cool on the baking sheet; it will be soft when it first comes out of the oven but will crisp up as it cools.

Grilled Cheese Sandwich

Ingredients:

- 1 tablespoon unsalted butter, softened

- 1 teaspoons of clarified cannabutter per sandwich

- 8 slices crusty bread

- 4 slices cheddar

- 4 slices Gruyere cheese

- 1 tablespoon olive oil

Tools:

- Small bowl

- Large non-stick skillet

- Spatula

Procedure:

1. In a small bowl, combine the butter and cannabutter. Spread the mixture on all 8 slices of the bread.

2. Layer 1 slice of cheddar and 1 of Gruyere on the unbuttered side of 4 of the slices.

3. In a large non-stick skillet, heat the olive oil over medium heat.

4. Cook all 8 slices until the bread is golden brown and the cheese melts.

5. Pair top and bottom halves to make sandwiches, cut in half, and serve warm

Pro tip: Add sausage in between the slices of bread; Chorizo, pepperoni and salami are amazing with grilled cheese.

Garlic Ganja Bread

Ingredients:

- 1 16-ounce loaf of Italian bread or French bread

- 1/2 cup clarified Cannabutter

- 2 large cloves of garlic, smashed and minced

- 1 heaping tablespoon of freshly chopped parsley

- 1/4 cup freshly grated Parmesan cheese

Tools:

- Sturdy Baking pan

Procedure:

1. Preheat oven to 350°F.

2. Cut the bread in half, horizontally.

3. Mix the Cannabutter, garlic, and parsley together in a small bowl. Spread butter mixture over the two bread halves.

4. Place on a sturdy baking pan (one that can handle high temperatures, not a cookie sheet) and heat in the oven for 10 minutes.

5. Remove pan from oven. Sprinkle Parmesan cheese over bread if you want.

6. Return to oven on the highest rack.

7. Broil on high heat for 2-3 minutes until the edges of the bread begin to toast and the cheese (if you are using cheese) bubbles. Watch very carefully while broiling. The bread can easily go from un-toasted to burnt.

8. Remove from oven, let cool a minute.

9. Remove from pan and make 1-inch thick slices. Serve immediately.

Pro tip: add more cheese, especially Gorgonzola.

Cannabis infused Drinks

One of the easiest and quickest methods to edibles or better said drinkables, with a long history over time with usage in India and China, I grew up knowing some of the possibilities and made my first marijuana tea around the age of 16, cannamilk and hot infused chocolate soon followed, basically every drink where THC has a chance to bind itself to fat has the potential to be infused, you could put a spoon of decarbed kief in a glass of water but I don't know if that has much effect as I never had the pleasure to try this out. What I do know is that you should never underestimate the power of putting hash in full fat chocolate milk, very easy to make but packs a punch, make your hash as powdery as possible, put it in the oven on 220F for about 45 minutes to decarb your product and put in in your full fat chocolate milk, next up is having the chocolate milk simmer just around boiling point for 30 minutes and you're good to go.

Cannabis Ghee Chai

Ingredients:

- 1 teaspoon potent clarified cannabutter
- ¾ cup pre-made tea of your choice (lemon is recommended)
- 2 cups water
- 4 cups milk
- ¼ cup sugar
- 1 inch cinnamon stick
- 6 cloves
- 6 green cardamom pods, cracked
- 6 black peppercorns
- 1 tsp. fresh minced ginger
- 1 tsp. oil
- ¼ cup half-and-half cream

Tools:

- Medium-sized cooking pot
- Cheese Cloth
- Mason Jar with lid

Procedure:

1. Put the clarified cannabutter, water, milk, sugar, cinnamon, cloves, cardamom, peppercorns, ginger and oil in a pan and bring to a boil.

2. Once boiling, lower the flame and let simmer for 15-20 minutes or until the Bhang becomes really fine and blended well.

3. Let it cool, strain the mixture with a cheese cloth into a jar, and keep it covered.

4. Pour ¼ cup of half-and-half cream and ¾ cup of strained tea in a cup. Heat it in the microwave and serve.

Mary Jane's Marijuana Tea

Ingredients:

- 1 Bag of tea per person

- 1 teaspoon of cannabutter per person

Procedure:

1. Add the 1 tsp. of clarified cannabutter and tea bag to the cup.

2. Boil the water and pour it in

3. Let the cannabutter fully dissolve.

4. Remove the tea bag, add milk if you like it, and consume

Pro tip: Add mint, cinnamon, ginger, lemon and other tasty things to your liking. Try out a pinch of black pepper, it might sound weird but it's my personal favourite.

Cannabis infused Chocolate Milk

Ingredients:

- Full fat Chocolate milk

- 1 teaspoon of Clarified cannabutter or about 1/5 of a gram hash

- Whipped cream

- Chocolate sprinkles

Tools:

- Small cooking pot

- Whisk

Procedure:

1. Decarb your hash if you're using that first, put it in a powdery, broken up form in the oven on 220F for about 30-45 minutes, depending on how much you're using.

2. Put your full fat Chocolate milk into a small cooking pot on your stove and bring it up to around boiling point on low heat.

3. Add your teaspoon of cannabutter or 1/5 of a gram of hash and let it fully dissolve.

4. If you're using cannabutter it is done by now, don't drink it while it is piping hot.

5. If you're using hash you need to let it simmer for about 30 minutes, keep it just around boiling point at a low heat.

6. Serve in a cup with whipped cream and chocolate sprinkles on top.

Pro tip: Add cannabutter and forget how much hash you're using so when it hits you, you'll be blasted into outer space. I did this and I'll never forget that.

Other books by HMPL Publishing

CBD has the power to change lives, health, and minds for the better. Marijuana, once a controversial substance, is made up out of 482 active components of which some have tremendous influential powers. With the recent acknowledgment of the healing powers of marijuana and its active component cannabidiol (CBD), the future of hemp oil and medical marijuana looks very bright. Not just bright for those in business, but more for those who have been suffering.

CBD & Hemp Oil: Cannabis, Cannabinoids and the Benefits of Medical Marijuana

Are you interested in Aaron's work about CBD? Grab the book here for only $0.99 (prices are subject to change).

http://amzn.to/2lmdVUz

Learn how to do it yourself. Make Hash, Cannabis oil, Rosin, BHO and other various types of hash, cannabis oil and other cannabis extracts right in the comfort of your home. Stop depending on your dispensary and start producing your own concentrates.

Beyond Cannabis Extracts: The Handbook to DIY Concentrates, Hash and Original Methods for Marijuana Extracts

Are you interested in Aaron's work about Cannabis Extracts?
Grab the book here for only $0.99 (prices are subject to change).

http://amzn.to/2mlTlnd

Learn how to do it yourself. Make Hash, Cannabis oil, Rosin, BHO and other various types of hash, cannabis oil and other cannabis extracts right in the comfort of your home. Stop depending on your dispensary and start producing your own concentrates.

Medical Marijuana: The Basic Principles For Cannabis Medicine

Are you interested in Aaron's work about Cannabis Extracts?
Grab the book here for only $0.99 (prices are subject to change).

http://amzn.to/2nwFlI7

Free Bonus

Don't forget to grab your free copy of 'The best DIY THC & CBD recipes to prepare at home'

http://eepurl.com/cxpVZf

Subscribe to the HMPL Publishing newsletter, and we'll give you our free THC & CBD recipes to prepare at home book for free.

All you have to do is enter your email address to get instant access.

We don't like spam and understand you don't like spam either. We'll email you no more than 2 times per week. Here are some of the things you can expect as a subscriber to HMPL Publishing's newsletter:

- The latest books by HMPL Publishing, exclusive and free for subscribers

- Delicious recipes to prepare in the comfort of you own kitchen

- Exclusive marijuana-related lectures, articles and information

- Special discounts for detailed eBooks about marijuana

- And much, much more...

To subscribe: **http://eepurl.com/cxpVZf**

You can also follow us on Facebook;

https://www.facebook.com/HMPLpublishing

Thank you

Finally, if you enjoyed this book, then I'd like to ask you for a small favour. Would you be kind enough to leave an honest review for this book on Amazon? It'd be greatly appreciated by both the future reader and me!

Thank you and good luck!